BOOK 1
PRINCESS IMMI, THE PROTECTOR

BOOK SERIES: IMMI AND TJ, THE ISLAND PROTECTORS

Written By
IMARA N. ARCHER AND INDIRA KINGLOCKE-ARCHER

Illustrated By
PUMUDI GARDIYAWASAM

© Copyright (2022) - Indira Kinglocke-Archer All rights reserved.

It is not legal to reproduce, duplicate, or transmit any part of this document in either electronic means or printed format. Recording of this publication is prohibited.

In a mystical land that rises on the Atlantic Ocean, a seven-hundred island chain of tranquil beauty, undersea mountains, and caves lived two brave children, Immi, and TJ.

The adventure began on a Saturday morning, the rising sun was peeping through a cloud, and Mr. Potbelly, a friendly Bahama parrot, was chirping at the children's bedroom window. "It's morning. It's morning, rise and shine. It's morning." Mr. Potbelly sang in a rake and scrape melody.

"Mommy, Daddy, we are ready!" Immi screamed, rushing to give her parents a big hug.

"Okay, children it's beach time," Dad said with a smile.

Mom, Dad, Immi & TJ would go to Coral Beach on Saturdays. This was a place where the golden sun sparkled on the water, seashells rested on sandy shores and the gentle warm breeze always danced with the palm trees.

The children loved the ocean. It was so clear that they could see all the beautiful sea animals, like a Nassau grouper hiding from a lionfish, a herd of seahorses marching, and baby stingrays catching waves.

At times, it made Immi sad that despite the beauty of Coral Beach, it was sometimes littered with plastics, bottles, and trash.

As soon as the family arrived at the beach, TJ dived into the turquoise waters while Immi collected the trash and placed it into a huge sack bag.

All of a sudden, while removing plastic from the seashore, Immi noticed something in the sand, a glowing pink feather. "Wow! This is beautiful!" Immi said, looking at the feather. Then she noticed another one. And another. And another.

Immi picked up each feather going down the beach until she saw the most amazing sight. A majestic flamingo was drinking water at a nearby pond, but the left leg was trapped in a huge plastic wrapper.

Immi left everything and rushed to help.

"I see that you are stuck. Are you okay? Oh, I know you cannot talk." Immi said as she removed the plastic wrapper from the flamingo's leg and placed it with the other trash.

She then pulled out a piece of cloth, dipped it in a bush medicine mixture from her backpack and bandaged the hurt leg.

"There you go, all better. Like my Nana always says, 'There aren't many things my Cerasee plant can't cure.' " Immi said in a calming voice just like her grandmother.

"Immi and TJ, come inside before it gets dark," Her mother called out from a distance.

"Bye flamingo, it's getting late, I must leave now," Immi said as she ran towards her mother.

The next Saturday, Immi was at the beach with her family. TJ was busy making sandcastles, Dad was taking a nap by the sea grape tree, Mom was fishing, and she was beach cleaning.

"Look, my sandcastle looks like a shark. Aaah!" TJ shouted pretending to be a shark.

"Hello, Princess Immi, the protector," a deep rough voice said suddenly from behind Immi.

It was the same flamingo from before.

"You can talk?" Immi said, surprised.

"Princess, all animals can talk but only with humans we trust. My name is Taino of the Filly Mingo Colony of Great Inagua Island." the flamingo answered.

Immi's face suddenly lit up with joy. "Taino? How do you know my name? Why did you call me Princess and the Protector?" She asked in excitement.

"That's a lot of questions, Princess Immi, but there's no time to answer them all, our islands need your help!" the flamingo said.

Immi became worried, "Tell me what I can do to help!" Immi asked.

"Hop on my back. We have a long journey ahead, I will take you to Lucaya, the oldest and wisest turtle of our islands. She will give you the answers you need." Taino said as Immi jumped on his back.

Immi held on tightly to Taino's neck as they flew over the Exuma Cays. In the sea below pigs were swimming, giggling, and flapping their ears.

"Taino, I can't believe my eyes! I never saw swimming pigs before!" Immi said laughing

"Princess Immi, there is no place in the world like our islands," Taino said.

As they arrived in the Exuma Cays, Immi stepped on something squishy.

"Ouch! Well, muddoes!" a squeaky voice yelled. Immi stepped back quickly, but she could not see anything in the sand.

"Taino, did you hear that?" she whispered.

"Oh, don't worry, it's just Tingum," Taino said.

Tingum was a purple iguana with three bulging yellow eyes, a sharp beak, rough skin, and a long curly tail. He was very clumsy. Immi found it so funny that a huge iguana could have such a squeaky voice.

"Just Tingum? I could've been smashed into a million pieces! Yinna mix right up, Bey." Tingum said in anger as he shook the sand off his body.

"Then stop hiding in the sand, you're not a chameleon," Taino said as he marched off.

Tingum sadly walked away.

"I am so sorry, I stepped on you, Tingum, I did not see you. Are you okay? I am Immi from the island of Grand Bahama." Immi said.

Tingum lit up with curiosity and tumbled high in the air, "You mean to tell me now, Princess Immi, the protector is here!" he shouted in excitement.

Immi shrugged her shoulders. She did not know why they would call her, a Princess, and a protector. Tingum began to walk and talk with her. He told Immi about the time he rescued his entire village from a creature called a Chick Charney.

"The beast was wild with red piercing eyes, three fingers, three toes, a half man, and half owl with a bushy tail, he was B-I-G, big but you know I aine never scared," said Tingum.

Tingum made Immi laugh, as he spoke about how he wrestled the Chick Charney to the ground.

"Princess with my little pinky claw, I threw that Chick Charney back into the pine forest of Andros Island," said Tingum.

The journey to Lucaya took Immi, Taino and Tingum through a mysterious cave with icicle-shaped blue crystals hanging from the ceiling. The walls of the caves were filled with artwork of the Arawak people.

"Bey, Taino you bring me into this cave to get me lost? You are a real trapsy! You know I don't like the dark. Um, I meant the dark hurts my eyes," said Tingum as he shook in fear.

"No Tingum, I brought you along because I know iguanas can see very well in the dark," replied Taino.

Suddenly a lightning bug with fiery wings dashed in their direction and sang, "Out of the dark and into the light, narrow is the way that leads to light. Come and follow me to the Blue Hole!"

Immi, Taino and Tingum followed the path of glittering light which led to the outside of the cave. When they arrived in the village, the lightning bug disappeared into the sky.

"Look! There is something dark in the water. It looks like poison." Taino said.

"This is not good. It is an oil spill." Immi said.

"I know one thing, these mosquitos here look bigger than me," Tingum said.

Immi heard a faint cry and saw a baby dolphin covered in thick oil gasping for air in the Blue Hole. "Oh, no!" Immi screamed as she ran to the rescue.

Immi held on to a coco plum branch to reach the dolphin.

"Princess! Be careful of the currents in the Blue Hole. There is a waterspout ahead if you go in, you will never return!" Taino shouted.

Immi tugged and pulled until she dragged the baby dolphin out of the oily water. The dolphin coughed as Immi slowly loosened her tight grip while cleaning off the oil.

Out of the sand, appeared a sea turtle with the map of The Bahamas painted on her shell. She slowly walked towards Immi.

My name is Lucaya. I am the oldest turtle on these islands. I have been waiting for you for a very long time, You are indeed our Princess, the Island Protector, the descendant of Chief, Aguma Awa." Lucaya said.

"Please, Lucaya, tell me. What does all of this mean?" Immi asked.

"Chief Aguma Awa told the story of the Yoruba people and how he was taken by Portuguese slave traders from his kingdom in Africa and brought to The Bahama Islands. The human traders came in large canoes with weapons that made fire and sailed across the Atlantic Ocean. They brought him to Vendue House in Nassau town. At this place, the traders took off his royal necklace and shackled him to a name, 'Guilleam Rahming.' " Lucaya said.

"Every August, my family go to Fox Hill Village Day. A celebration of the Emancipation which ended slavery. Our festival is a time of unity, people from all over our islands come together as one. There we remember our ancestors and celebrate freedom." Immi said.

"Those human traders changed our Chief's name but could not change his destiny. Chief Awa always walked with his head held high, knowing that he once ruled as king. A brave protector of our islands and he was a loved leader in Fox Hill Village. " said Lucaya.

"Wow! My ancestor was a king, from the Yoruba tribe of Africa. That will make me a Princess." Immi said filled with pride.

"This is your heritage, your ancestry, your legacy," Lucaya said.

"Please, tell me how did the oil enter the Blue Hole?" Immi asked.

"Three sunrises ago, I heard the cry of corals. As I swam nearby to take a closer look, I saw a human riding on a large nose yellow dragon removing our precious sand near the coral reef. The dragon fell and left this poison in the water." Lucaya answered.

"That was no dragon that you saw, it was a yellow sand drilling machine. This is horrible! Coral reefs are important to our ecosystems." Immi said.

"Princess, do humans care that they are causing great harm to our islands?" Lucaya asked.

"I do not think many humans realize that we do not have another earth to live on. No Planet B exists! This oil can leave the Blue Hole and harm other habitats." Immi cried.

"Come closer to me and listen. Princess, I sent Taino to find you. A long, long time ago when our waters were pure, our precious sand was pink, when the crocodiles lived in mangroves and the pine forest filled the land, the elders of these islands spoke of a brave little girl, who will help to protect our islands." Lucaya said.

"Who Me? It just couldn't be. I'm just one little island girl." Immi said.

"Princess, there is great danger ahead. As I closed my eyes to sleep, I saw waters coming out of ice mountains flow from a faraway and swallowed our Bahama land.' Lucaya said.

"Oh, Lucaya! You dreamt about climate change, this is causing the ice to melt in the Arctic. The pollution in the air is causing our earth to get hotter, and the Artic ice is melting and can cause harm to our islands with rising waters." Immi said.

"You have greatness on the inside you. " Lucaya said.

"Princess, look around and tell me what you see?" Lucaya asked.

As Immi looked around, her eyes widened in surprise.

"I see the queen conch, tiger sharks, spiny lobsters, land crabs, corals, jellyfish, a barracuda, spotted dolphins, starfish and a shiny blue marlin with a goombay drum dancing to the sounds of Junkanoo," Immi said.

Princess Immi, Taino, Tingum and all of the sea animals were all dancing together.

"You are not alone," Taino said.

"Forward! Upward! Onward! Together!" Tingum shouted as he clumsily fell, and everyone laughed.

Immi was happy to meet her new friends.

"I believe I can help to protect our islands and I know just the right human to join us," Immi said thinking about her brother, TJ.

Taino flew Immi back to Coral Beach near her home. She waved goodbye as the flamingo ran forward, flapped his wings, and took off into the air.

Then Immi heard her dad's voice from a distance, "Immi and TJ, come let's go! We need to prepare there is a monster hurricane coming in the east wind!" Dad shouted.

"Immi, where did you go?" TJ asked.

"Ssh! TJ, I will tell you everything, promise," Immi whispered.

"Daddy, we are on our way." Immi and TJ said.

Back home everyone was busy battening up windows, pulling down shutters, stacking up sandbags, and preparing for the worst but hoping for the best.

Immi and T.J.'s adventures as The Island Protectors had only just begun.

TO BE CONTINUED...

MAP OF THE BAHAMAS
THE ISLAND PROTECTOR MAP

- Little Abaco
- Grand Bahama
- Great Abaco
- Berry Islands
- Bimini Islands
- Eleuthera
- New Providence
- Andros
- Cat Island
- San Salvador
- Rum Cay
- The Exumas
- Long Island
- Crooked Island
- Ragged Island
- Acklins Island
- Mayaguana Island
- Little Inagua
- Great Inagua

0 — Miles — 100

20

Glossary – The Island Protector's Facts

Arawak people are the first recorded natives of the Bahamas, also known as Tainos and Lucayans.

Archipelago is a group of islands in the ocean or sea.

The Arctic region is one of the coldest places on earth and is centred on the North Pole. Huge mountains of ice called icebergs float on the Arctic Ocean.

Bahama Parrot is also called the Abaco parrot, known for having a white head and mostly green body.

Bey is a Bahamian slang word for a person.

Blue hole is a circle shape sinkhole usually near an underwater cave system that may connect a freshwater lake to the ocean.

Bush medicine are native plants found in The Bahamas that are used to cure and heal.

Cay is a little low island made of sand, coral, or rock.

Cerasee is a vine-like green plant with a yellow flower and it is prepared to cure ailments in The Bahamas.

Climate Change means the difference in Earth's atmosphere (the gas layer surrounding Earth). The climate changes.

Coastal Area is the area where land meets the sea or ocean.

Coco plum plant is found near water; it grows a delicious native fruit.

Coral reefs are large underwater homes for tiny sea creatures called corals.

Currents are water moving in the same direction.

Ecosystem is the home for all living and nonliving things in an area. This can mean plants, animals, and other types of living things.

Endangered species are animals or plants that are seriously at risk of extinction.

Flamingo is the national bird of The Bahamas. The world's largest colony of West Indian pink flamingos live on the island of Inagua at the National Park.

Fox Hill is one of the oldest villages on New Providence Island, where liberated Africans from various tribes settled.

Goombay is the official Bahamian music and the native Goombay drum is used to create the melody of Junkanoo.

Habitat is the environment of an animal.

- Hurricane is a storm with fierce winds.

- Junkanoo is a cultural festival of vibrant costumes, lively music, and street dancing. This connects with African identity.

- Mangrove is a tree with roots in the water which are above the ground and grows along the coasts.

- Meltwater is water released by the melting of snow, ice, or iceberg caused by the heating of the earth.

- Muddoes is a word used by the natives of The Bahamas as an expression of excitement, fear, or displeasure.

- Pollution is anything that can cause harm to the environment.

- Portugal is a country in Europe. The Trans-Atlantic Slave Trade began when Portuguese traders brought the first large number of slaves from Africa.

- Potbelly is to be shaped with a swollen stomach.

- Queen Conch is a large yellowish conch, a mollusc with a hard smooth shell.

- Rake-and-Scrape is the traditional music of The Bahamas. It has the sound of African musical elements and uses a saw as the main instrument.

- Seagrass bed is a meadow underwater where sea creatures live.

- Swimming Pigs in The Bahamas swim every day in the ocean. Islanders say they were perhaps left by shipwreck sailors years ago.

- Tingum is a Bahamian word used when one cannot remember the name of a person, place, or thing.

- Trapsy is a term used for a person who is always setting traps and not to be trusted.

- Vendue House is located on Bay Street, Nassau where slaves were sold and auctioned in The Bahamas during the Eighteenth century.

- Waterspout near the blue hole is a dangerous fast-spinning circular flow of water.

- Yoruba is an African ethnic group. In Fox Hill Village, in New Providence Island, Liberated Africans formed the Yoruba Society in The Bahamas.

- Yinna mix right up is a phrase expressing a state of confusion.

www.ingramcontent.com/pod-product-compliance
Lightning Source LLC
LaVergne TN
LVHW070611080526
838200LV00103B/343